A Crack Between the Worlds

Poems from the White Island

Yabisa Gashouse Anthology 2018

Published by
YABISA GASHOUSE
C/ R. Curtoys Gotarredona, 1, Esc. 2, 2B
07840 Santa Eulària des Riu
Spain

Compiled and edited by Robert Hale.
Copyright © Robert Hale 2019.

Cover artwork and all illustrations © Pere Vergés Coma 2018.
With thanks to Paloma Cabezas for the cover layout.

ISBN: 978-84-949638-0-3

Find our poetry at:
www.yabisagashouse.tumblr.com
www.instagram.com/yabisagashouse
www.facebook.com/yabisagashouse

Foreword

This collection of verse derives from a small project which has evolved organically amongst a group of like-minded people living on the island of Ibiza. It began with small gatherings where music would be played, poetry read, and philosophising engaged in (for which one might with some justification read "nonsense talked"), instigated by one of our number (Pere Vergés Coma). When I started putting our poems on the Internet, a name was needed. Yabisa (or Yebisah) is the old Moorish name for Ibiza[1]. The Gas House was a venue in Los Angeles in the 1950s where poets and other artists would meet and share their work and ideas. The two names were put together and *Yabisa Gashouse* was born.

Each chapter of the book presents poems by a different author. Within each chapter the poems are sequenced in order of the date when they were written, except where it is the author's preference or there are other special reasons to sequence them differently.

A minor note about British/American spelling: our group has members of various nationalities, all writing in English. Thus both British and American spellings are found in these poems.

We hope you enjoy our poetry.

Santa Eulària des Riu, Eivissa, 28/12/18.

---

1   Ibiza has had various names through the ages: Ibossim (Phoenicians), Ebusus (Romans), Pityûssai (the ancient Greek name for Ibiza and Formentera, meaning "pine-covered islands") from which derives the modern name Pitiusas, Yebisah or Yabisa (Moors), Eivissa (the name in the local language, Eivissenc, a dialect of Catalan), and the "White Island" (hence our subtitle), name of uncertain origin but possibly deriving from the traditionally white colour of the houses. In Ibiza today, both Spanish and local (Catalan) place names are current. From this point on in the notes, in respect for local custom, we have chosen to use the local names. Thus, for example, Eivissa for Ibiza.

Wings of Wine

Heavy were the glasses, though
They were empty when they came;
As I lit them in the flame
Of pure wine, and let it grow

Suddenly they grew so light
That they seemed about to soar,
As the body, gross before
Flutters with the new-born sprite.

Ibn al-Yamani.[2]
Translated by A. J. Arberry.[3]

---

2   Idris ibn al-Yamani was a Moorish poet living in Ibiza during the 11th century.

3   A. J. Arberry. Moorish Poetry: A Translation of The Pennants, an Anthology compiled in 1243 by the Andalusian Ibn Sa'id. Copyright © Cambridge University Press 1953. Extract reproduced with permission of Cambridge University Press.

Contents

To Calliope, Erato, Euterpe, Polihymnia,
and Thalia, Greek Muses of poetry.

Helen Gosch

Arrival to Ibiza

Lying under the pyramid
Soft Ibicencan mood surrounds
Love, far away
Love, near
Consciousness encompasses the all

Life is no more than a series of rooms
Each door opens a new view
A new vibration
A new self
Each room has furnishings designed for the
      moment

Each door has a special key
The password must be learned
The trials endured
Tests overcome
The door behind disappears into some
      forgotten dream

The moment determines the color
The color is the clue
Go with the color of the room
Close and open doors when they come
Sit in the chair when sitting time arrives

The yellow deep color of the Earth
Blends with the grounding one feels in the
      legs
The azure blue sky

The reflection in the sea
Flies the spirit toward eternity

This room has no walls
The color is pale
Its furnishings transparent
The door is no more than a cloth in the breeze

A bird circling overhead
Calls for it's mate to join
To fly
To soar beyond the limits of reality

I stand and look
At the body
In this room
And I know
It is true

Can Pep Ramon, Sant Augustí des Vedrà, February
1981.

Pyramedia

The moon beams
High above the world
Full, golden, pure.
The lover sleeps,
The child dreams,
The fire embers ooze
Quietly through the night.
I float gently through the scene
Warming to the sounds.
The wheel begins to turn.
New life evolves, naturally,
Unharassed.
A true life,
An unfoldment.
The old is in a pyramid,
Experiences learned.
A circle lies ahead.
Unending, yet unturned,
A spiral is the way.
The yearning for the new,
A dawning of the day.

Can Pep Ramon, Sant Augustí des Vedrà, February
1981.

Moonlight Love

You discovered a space in me
Like the moon found space in the window.
I was closed, battened down,
As the window's wooden shutter is
Designed to keep the world out.

Then, along you came
With the moon rising over the mountain,
Discovering the slit in my life
Through which love might shine
Like golden rays of moonlight
Slipping through a shutter-slat accidentally
		left askew.

I didn't mean to find love.
The sliver of moonbeam
Lying on the carpet
Didn't mean to discover
My inner-most desire.

The day slips our love
Back to the recesses of dream.
The moon fades in the sunlight.
But it is there clearly
On the other side of the world
Burning unseen to those around us
Ready to come again the moment
The twilight starts to sing its evening song.

Love comes over the mountainside

Into my awaiting arms.
The moon plays across my breast
Joins our kissing lips.
My lover plays on his trombone.
Can life be more than this, O master?

Can Pep Ramon, Sant Augustí des Vedrà, March 1981.

Advice for the Young

Consider the February almond flower.
Pick it to delight the senses
And you have it for a day.

Pick the soft green fuzzy fruit
Of early April and you have
Sensuous delight for a week.

Fruit turns sour and brown
When too early picked.
Wait till it falls freely
From the tree in its own time
By its own nature, ripe.

The rich brown flavorful almond nut
Will stay with you through
The winter of your life,
To be eaten slowly and delicately
Until the warm soft spring comes again.

Nor hurry the cycles of life
Or the seasons of nature.
It is never too late.

This I know you will understand.

Can Pep Ramon, Sant Augustí des Vedrà, 1981.

Unfinished Finished

My love is like a flower field,
Varied hues all blending,
Gentle leaves and sturdy lips,
And in the wind they're bending.

I sit for a while with the gentle folk,
To contemplate their love,
They speak to me in whisperers,
And many colored moods.

As I wander through the fields,
The flowers close their faces,
And I look upon the moon,
In one of its glorious phases.

I walk in the night undaunted,
Unchanged and never failing,
With an endlessness in my heart,
Of burning love, never paling.

The sky is full of falling stars,
Shooting from all directions,
The senses open to the change,
And I feel a deep connection.

The flowers of the field have gone,
Replaced by memories,
The gentle leaves and sturdy lips,
Blend in reverie.

Tell the gentle folk,

The whisperings are held,

I speak out loud,

To my new flight,

And walk off into the moonlight.

Unfinished 12 April 1981 Can Pep Ramon, Sant Augustií des Vedra.

Finished 13 August 2009, Can Puig, Sant Augustií des Vedra.

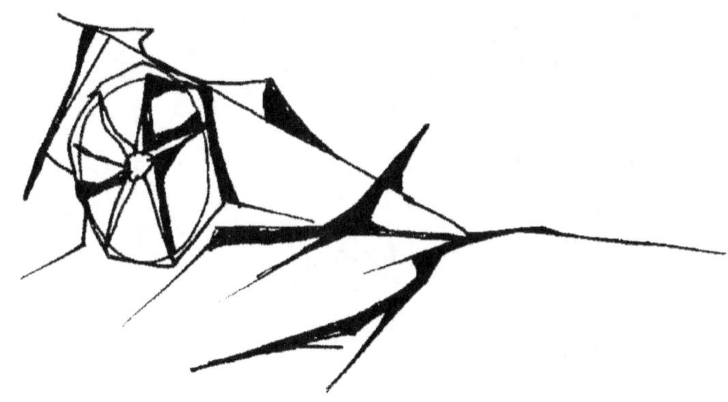

The Bayonet

Why?
Men make war
Increase their power
Land and possessions
Domination and control
Politics and ideologies.

Masters brainwash boys
Do before done to
Fear, fear
Enter the unthinkable
Cut, smash, burn
Destroy and kill.

Rape
In the height of battle
Weaken the enemy
Strike at its treasure
Total annihilation
Infiltrate seed
Children changed forever.

Excuses, excuses
Untamed forces rise
Lauded fantasy
Defenseless victim
Cowering in corner
Covering children.

Thick hard drive
Overwhelms rationality
Procreate before death
Ecstatic bliss
Biological weapon
Woman dripping on the floor.

Frozen children stare
Then they cry
Loud and shrill
Purpose of bayonet
To kill
To kill

Sant Augustí des Vedrà, 2018.[4]

____

4   When I was 16 my first puppy-love boyfriend enlisted in the US Marines.
During his first visit home after boot camp he told me something about his
training: the purpose the bayonet. I will never forget it.

Prose Poem

Once upon a time there was born
in a very, very large and very, very flat
       country
a blue-eyed girl child.
As far as the eye could see,
anyone who looked would find oceans
of high stalks of golden ears of corn.
The girl grew with her heart full,
full of innocence and joy,
running freely in the wind,
her heart beating wildly under the sun.
Then came the idea.
The idea that the mountains and the forests
and the sea also could give innocence and joy.
She took her full heart and her golden
       memories
of a land clean and free and moved on.
She traveled where she had never imagined
       she would ever go.
She saw many kinds of things and met many
       people who spoke strange words
and with their eyes told stories of ideas she
       had never known.
She traveled and she saw,
until the innocence became knowledge
and the joy became wisdom.
She never settled, she never returned.
She wandered with her eyes open
and her heart ready to beat wildly under any
       sun.

The day she died she was nowhere and
     everywhere.
Light was pouring into her heart and out of
     her eyes.
She ascended into another place,

very, very large and very, very flat,

with high stalks of golden corn as far as the
     eye could see.

From my Mediterranean island I look at the
     sky.
To sunset hues of blue and purple,

to an unending variety of clouds.

When I hang my laundry the wind reminds me
     of miles and miles of cornfields.
Am I the same?

Quadrillions of seconds I have lived in this
     universe,
living it, thinking it, dreaming it as I went
     along,
following from one place to another, going
     with the flow.

The softness of the sunset has always captured
     my heart.

I look away from the falling sun into the
     eastern clouds.
Hills reflect the changing light,

the sun, brightly off the houses on the hill

with a hazy green background and a pale blue
     sky.
The golden yellow of the wheat field,

the dark sap green of the fig.

A swallow and a bat start their nightly feed,
pesky mosquitoes swarm up from the balsa.
The cat, fed, lazes around before the nightly
      hunt.

Nature integrated.

Houses, chiseled out of the landscape,
dramatic strong white against shadow.
The whiskey glass empties as my heart
      becomes fuller,
fuller with nature's temping gifts.
How can such romanticism come from a glass
      of sour mash?
Look West.
Clouds, illuminated on the western edge,
are dark, rainy dark on the eastern.
A golden glow near the sea blends into the
      fading sky.

Oh, I move to see the descending sun,
so far north that I can't even find it.
At my famous washing line a strong shining
      orb
blinds me as it sinks into the great puddle of
      Mediterranean.
Gloaming descends, wind stills,
Venus appears, mirrored in the sea.
I wander back to the house in the cooling air,
pet the cat a bit. Contentment washes over
      me.

Sant Augustí des Vedrà, 2018.

To My Coy Mistress

Alone on the pillow,
Warm, vanilla-pale,
Your limbs reach out to me.
Volumes of curves, smooth,
Soft to touch, easy to see.

Hidden under the skin,
Memories live deep
In those spaces between
Volumes of curves, smooth,
Existing in your dream.

Memories of loves,
Pains, caresses, and bumps,
Create now what you are,
Volumes of curves, smooth,
Forming your beautiful aura.

How I love your form,
Your lines come off my pen,
Like ideas for a poem.
Volumes of curves, smooth,
As I draw your simple pose.

Light flows around you,
Floating on the cushion,
Like the sunlight of your face.
Volumes of curves, smooth,
Ever vibrant in your space.

To my coy mistress,
My model for life,
You captured my heart.
Volumes of curves, smooth,
I drowned in my art.

Immortality
Seduced my artist mood
To preserve forever,
Volumes of curves, smooth,
The treasure of womanhood.

Sant Augustí des Vedrà, 2018.[5][6]

---

5   Title inspired by Andrew Marvell, *To His Coy Mistress*, published in 1681, three years after his death. Andrew Marvell is known today as one of the English metaphysical poets writing on subjects such as man's place in the universe, existence, love and religion.

6   The drawing accompanying this poem is by the poem's author (Copyright © Helen Gosch 2018).

Pulled into the World

Her mother was grateful for the rain,
For even in the early morning…
The still dark early morning
Of a hot and clammy August,
Louise thought she had sweated
All the sweat that existed
For months of humid Iowa summer
Carrying around this great heat inside.
Her mother immensely disliked heat,
Pined for winter's isolating snow banks,
Freezing chilled wind. This morning,
    however,
She was pulled into the world hot,
An explosion of human existence,
And her mother immediately felt the cool,
    dark air of 1940.

I can imagine the awe felt
In the hands of all that is warm and beautiful.
And the first thing I saw when my eyes
    cleared
Was the blue light radiance of my older
    sister's eyes
As she gazed upon me in wonder.

Sant Augustí des Vedrà, 2018.

At the Airport

Lately I find myself at the airport.
I've not checked in at all
And I'm not in the departure lounge,
I've only just arrived at the terminal.

But I'm thinking about where I want to go.
Or which destinations are available.
What's going to happen if I leave this place?
It's all so big and un-understandable.

Will my family be there to greet me?
Show me my new style of life?
Or will angels with wings guide me to bliss?
Or worse....will there be strife?

Shall I go to the Karmic lounge,
Await for the floor to be swept,
Till I can be suitably charged
For my life of cause and effect.

Or to face my Lord at the Gate,
Pearly with golden gilt,
With fear churning the gut
From childhood religious guilt.

There's an assembly hall where I can wait
The arrival of the others,
When the sky will open and a terrible
Voice will call me and my brothers.

Up through the Astral, Mental, Causal
Can I fly my soul higher
Toward planes of consciousness
To become God's co-worker?

Have I gained enlightenment enough
To return to this beautiful place,
Or move as a spiritual guide
Somewhere out of physical space?

Should I disappear into the etheric,
The ocean of love and mercy,
To become one with all eternal,
A part of the cosmos energy?

Or do I just close my wizened eyes,
Slow my earthly heart and breath
Down into nothingness, nothingness,
And let there be peace in the valley of death.

Sant Augustí des Vedrà, 2018.

Life Is Life

LIFE requires a soft edge.
Changing, pulling, nothing fixed,
Life is life when it's changing.
Can one stand still and change? That's the
      secret.
Perhaps I'll learn the art.

How many years and lifetimes
I have stood still and changed,
Drifting FEARLESSLY along the stream,
Free not to plan, not to flow life.
Freed to let life flow me.

I will never say never. I will say
I discovered the creature within me
To love, called SELF. Don't call it a waste….
It's time well spent,
Learning to trust.

The outgoing tide laps forever
Incessantly against my ankles.
My heart reluctantly responds.
I pry my body away,
Knowing and sensing the whirlpool

Around the corner, sucking
Further and further into the dark mires of life.
I prefer to lie on top of the ocean,
Drying dew accumulated during the night.
Onwards I float, in an endless time stream.

The stars are my guidelines.
My limits transparently thin.
Spirit supports me in full.
The ocean waves hold my secrets
Tenderly dancing in their grasp.

I, you, we are the ocean,
The infinite OCEAN, holding infinity.
Fill it, but leave the door open,
Always room for more.
To close is to die,

To become an island
In the moving sea.
Take what you find there,
And give it your ALL.
Open your heart to everything.

The free soul
Flies above the world
In the clear, blue vibration of now.
Not using strength,
It flies on deep love,
With a well tuned flute to show it how.

A fine clear note
Draws up high the soul,
The heart opens and whispers low.
Waves of vibration
Join the lustrous vision
Of the freedom of a thousand souls.

Sant Augustí des Vedrà, 2018.

The Braided River

We come like braided rivers.
Different velocities creating
Multiple interweaving channels.
Slow moving on the inside of a bend
Our huddled masses come
Surging in outward migration,
An international odyssey,
One step at a time.
Yearning, yearning to breath free
From war strife, from life strife,
Moving like slow gravel and stone,
Over desert valleys, burning,
Walls of water, drowning,
Coming alone, with nothing but children.
Meandering where we can,
Filling an entire valley floor,
Spreading wide, making islands
In the existing landscape.

We come for a tangle of reasons
This convoy of migrants who
Won't stop, can't stop
With strollers and wheelchairs
We come not from choice
In sandals and dresses
With nothing to eat
But from need to survive the
Poverty, gangs, crime,
Violence, drought, systematic corruption,

Insecurity and death.

Braided rivers flowing,
Poor, impoverished refugees
On perilous journeys stream
Toward safe, affluent borders
Somewhere here on Planet Earth.

Sant Augustí des Vedrà, 2018.

About Helen Gosch

I was born in Iowa, USA. Life was simple and free.
I travelled around studying art, all the time learning to see.
Big cities and small, country after country,
I dwelt in strange places, even lived on the sea.
Life dealt me no bad cards, was easy on me,
And I found my true self, when I landed on I B Z.

26

27

Robert Hale

The Poets Are Gone

The house is empty
The door is barred
The windows boarded over
The poets are gone
Their words once bravely scrawled
Or painted brighter, bolder
Than the ordinary way
On an ordinary day
Are fading from the flaking walls
The poets have gone to the hills
Their pens are dry
Like the torrent beds
Of a parched July
It is said
Their thoughts have stopped
Like smoke in the air
Hanging over dark hilltops
The poets are gone, the house is bare
The lock is jammed with rust
The writing book is dust
There's nothing there
Any more
The poets have gone

Santa Eulària des Riu, June 2018.[7]

---

7   This poem is out of sequence (the rest in this section are in order of date). I have put it first because it is one reason why Yabisa Gashouse came into being. Eivissa has a history as a hive of artistic creativity. Rightly or wrongly, I felt that in recent years much of this had been lost. Or maybe, I considered, it had just gone to ground.

The World Through the Window

The curtains weave to a gentle push-pull
That through the open door brings in the night
Short-tempered waves crash and slide back
Thunder booms far out at sea
A soft, haunting symphony floats
From restless balcony chimes
Bar tables are moved, a rude chain
Is pulled around chair legs
A dog barks and is answered
A small neurotic motorbike
Whines frantic up the street
Laughing and joshing from the bench below
The Andalusian girls go clap, clap-clap
And cry out another anguished lament
As she and I lie wrapped
In our timeless world within

Santa Eulària des Riu, August 2011.[8]

---

8   The sounds of the outside world float through the open French window of
my room. There is a popular bar in the alleyway beneath the balcony, with
lively tables on the pavement outside, and beside them a public bench where
sometimes in summer children gather to practise their Flamenco.

Ways to the Sea

All paths lead to the sea but they ain't all easy
You might find an easy road but it won't be
    free
So I walk and I climb and I scrape till I get
    weary
Just to find what is waiting there for me
But what other way is there for it to be?

And you may find a hole which you can sleep
    in
And you may find a hole where the ground is
    hard
And you'll find to eat but the fruit ain't always
    juicy
And you may find to drink where the water's
    old
But what other way is there for it to be?

All our dead ends are just our limitations
No wings to fly way down this wild gulley
Where I'm sitting here to voice my
    incantations
Cicadas scream hypnotic from tree to tree
And what other way is there for it to be?

Cala d' Albarca, Sant Mateu d'Albarca, July 2015.[9]

---

9   I like to walk along the cliffs and shorelines of Eivissa's rugged north coast.
I composed this song while walking. I think it sounds good to the tune of
Bob Dylan's *Absolutely Sweet Marie.*

To Watch from the Mala Costa

To watch from the Mala Costa
At the birth time of the day,
The magic silent twilight burst;
The sun looks out to the western lay.
There, crowds will gather all in thirst,
To catch its glorious dying ray,
But I look East remembr'ing first
Another, solitary, silent way.

Sant Vicent, Sant Joan de Labritja, 2015.[10]

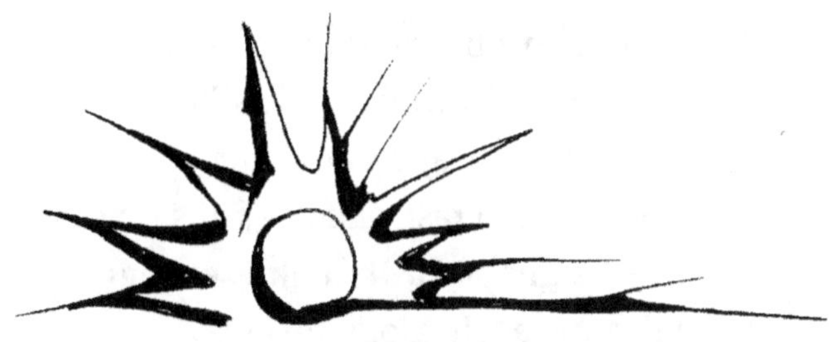

---

10 The Serra de la Mala Costa is a range of hills in the north-east of Eivissa, from whose eastern slopes one can watch the sun rising from beyond the sea. If you are up there at dawn, you will likely be the only one around; a bit of a different feel from the Café del Mar in Sant Antoni de Portmany, where people flock to watch the sun set.

The Back of the Bay

I woke up at the dawn of the day
And I wandered up a pine-wooded way,
Then took myself down to the back of the bay,
Where the crags are sharp and the sun does
    play,
In glitter bright on the sea and the spray,
That roll and toss in the mouth of the bay.

And the wind is up and the waves are large,
Their blue so dark as in fury they charge,
And the gulls in the sky chatter and dive,
And I feel so fine and I feel so alive,
As along the cliff I make my way,
With the waves and wind at the back of the
    bay.

They ask me if I believe God exists.
Well, I say I'll allow that He is all this.
I don't try to know and I don't make a fuss,
As the waves do crash and the gulls do cuss.
'Cause the sight of this I think is enough.
And I'll come again along this way,
That takes me down to the back of the bay.

Cala d'Albarca, Sant Mateu d'Albarca, June 2016.[11]

---

11 Poem also published in *Nature Writing* online magazine on 14/04/2018
(https://naturewriting.com/the-back-of-the-bay/).

Song to the Archetypal Forest

Today the spirit moves from the south;
the air is thick as I set out.
A hot wind fans this rugged land,
harsh and sweet as the desert sands.

I walk on ways where five years since,
high flames raged and the smoke was dense.
The pine trees burned, the birds flew fast;
all fled or died as the fire storm passed.

And when the flames were finally quenched
you saw a land where life was wrenched,
a smouldering waste, a landscape scarred,
stone walls scorched and tree stumps charred.

Yet even as people cried and railed
at the turns of fate, at certainties failed,
just as a fever will cleanse the flesh,
there's a force at work in the land afresh.

As I look on, five years hence,
on these ancient ways where pines were
     dense,
it's a strange, hard, beautiful, different world;
a new order begins to unfold.

Vital, clambering, fresh and strong:
a new world of colour and song.
I gaze on the hills in wonder and awe;
tenacity springs from every pore.

The archetypal forest's plan
is death and rebirth and to Hell with man's
other designs, his need to control,
ignoring the greater laws of old.

Large pines are gone, juniper too,
the land is rough, the trees are few.
The ones that stand are but hip height,
but all between, a glorious sight.

Now rosemary, lavender and rockrose reign,
butcher's broom and yellow fleabane,
wild thyme, heather, spiked ivy vine;
each singing a verse to the spirit's rhyme.

Sant Vicent, Sant Joan de Labritja, October 2016.[12] [13]

---

12 Fire is an ancient and physiological part of the forest ecosystem. This poem
    is about the fire which struck the north-east of Ibiza in 2011.
13 Poem also published in *Nature Writing* online magazine on 28/03/2018
    (https://naturewriting.com/song-to-the-archetypal-forest/).

The Watch

How many hours have my eyes gazed upon
Those towers that jut from the oily sea?
I see them even in the night,
Immobile, jagged, tall and free.
Yet what will they, then, tell of me?
I know each crag, every angle of their lean,
The depth of shadow of each hollow and fold.
Waiting, watching, hour and day,
I know every tone of grey and gold.
I'll know this, too, when all is done and told.

So long have my senses pricked and thrilled
To the tireless call of the restless waves
Which thrash in the fibres of my flesh,
Nervous, brooding, wild and brave.
What can they know, of these men in this
     cave?
I know the moods, the lines of flow,
The deep dark trough, the frothing crest.
Waiting, listening, through to morn,
I know the cold and the fear no less.
I'll know it, too, when all is laid to rest.

How long have you shrilled and slapped my
     skin,
You headstrong wind that curls on the brine?
On these autumn days, that turn to chill,
You impetuous, maddening, lover of mine,
Do you carry my scent with thine?
I've known your summer whispered charms,

Your winter raging shrieks and yells.
Waiting, feeling, with every cell,
I know every tale my lover tells.
I'll know it still, at the final bell.

So long we've conversed, in chatter and song,
You gulls that plane and dive and sing.
We know each other so well, so long,
White darts, you masters of the wing.
Do you know, do you see what fate will bring?
I know your voice, the turn of your flight,
Your clucks and cries, the marks on your bill.
Waiting, watching, through to dusk,
I see in your eyes your thoughts, your will.
I'll know it, too, when blood will spill.

Would that I know my foe so well,
For finding me, he'll shoot me dead.
We were kids together, friends at school,
But now he would shoot me through the head.
And the story never will be read,
And all this, all this that I know,
Those towers, the sea, the wind, the gulls,
He'll have known them, too, our time, our
            place,
The soil, the sea, the sky and all.
He'll know my world, when he too shall fall.

Sant Mateu d'Albarca, Eivissa, November 2016.[14]

---

14 On the rocky north coast of Eivissa there is a little known series of caves in a cliff face, of difficult access, where the men from the local village used to hide from the Guardia Civil during the Spanish Civil War of 1936-39. Sitting on a ledge outside this cave on a cloudy autumn day, overlooking a restless sea, I imagined what the thoughts of a man on guard duty might have been.

Remembrances (Men of Santa Agnès)

Sometimes, travelling slow,
When the rain falls softly through the leaves,
Or the clouds hang grey in dawn's pale glow,
Or when night is thick and the darkness
          breathes,
Or the morning mist on the plain hangs low,
Or when gulls circle high as a black sea
          heaves,
And the pines on the cliff stand grey in a row,
Sometimes, then, quick on the breeze,
Come whispered voices from long ago.

November, mellow and still,
Waves rolling pebbles down on the shore,
Smoke rising up, over the hill,
The mood hypnotic, the feeling raw.
The air is pregnant, a vacuum to fill;
My senses attune to the land and its lore.
Then I can see and then I can feel
Memories coming from mankind's store,
For a second, then gone again, leaving a chill.

Sometimes, travelling blind,
The stuff of the world will quiver and shift,
For a second, a minute, a trick of the mind,
The wind will drop and a veil will lift.
There... Hear their voices, quick on the wind.
The men, they are coming, bound for the cliff,
Their idiom strange, they sing as they climb,

"We go to the boats, we go to fish,
We'll come back this way, if Our Lady is
kind".

Santa Agnès de Corona, November 2016.[15]

---

15 Poem also published in *Nature Writing* online magazine on 07/11/2018 (https://naturewriting.com/remembrances/).

A Walk in Black and White

Along a white path upon a black night
Thoughts of the day all taking flight
A white thin moon hangs in a black sky
A star so bright travelling with it so high
A white heron hunts by the black of the sea
In its beak something silvery flaps to be free
A white bridge stands low, before a black hill
So many years so silent, so still
A white duck floats upon a black pool
Like a white pearl set against a black jewel

Santa Eulària des Riu, December 2016.[16]

---

16 Walking along the Santa Eulària seafront to the "river" mouth, then up the
creek to the old bridge on a winter's evening.

A Well Kept Garden

Yes, they may have had their ways,
Done, at times, as they would not
Be done by, committed trespasses
Small or large, born malice,
Spoken words unjust, which
From time to time, perhaps,
Went unconfessed on Sunday.
Yet the eyes of these folk are good
As they gaze from the sills
Of their cold polished slabs.

It is a well kept garden, this,
With its swept paths dividing
Neat flower beds and squares
Of trimmed and watered lawn.
A rake, a broom, a bin for cuttings
Tidily stored in a corner.
And orderly, terraced rows
Of fine multi-story accommodations
For the good folk of this town.

Adorned most with bright flowers -
Plastic (on discrete inspection),
But cheerful nevertheless.
Though some façades are faceless,
With no good eyes gazing out,
And slab-less too,
Just initials scrawled, and dates,
In crayon on concrete,

And a grubby plastic bloom
Lonely on the sill.

My footsteps sound on the path.
Children's shouts and shrieks
Filter through from the church front.
The quiet here is not soundless,
But of a deeper, more solid kind.
Sunlight glances down in beams
On these good, unseeing folk.
For rich and poor,
Cherished and forgotten,
It is a glad place to lie.

Santa Eulària des Riu, December 2016.[17] [18]

---

17 The cemetery adjoining the old Church on the hill above Santa Eulalia is a
    very peaceful place to stop, for a few minutes, or an eternity.
18 Poem first published in *Poetry Quarterly*, Issue 31 (Fall 2017), Prolific
    Press, 2018.

Line in Two Blues

A blob of orange-gold slides molten
Over the line in two blues
Where sea meets sky
On a January morning
Of crystal brilliance.
Taking form, it climbs the lesser blue
Warming my seaward side
As I walk.
A white heron, disturbed,
Launches heavily from the shallows
Trailing stalky legs,
Veering east.
A cormorant, nervous,
Cranes its neck,
Dives from its rock
To boisterous white tops
Licked by gusts of chill
From round Cap LLibrell.

Santa Eulària des Riu, January 2017.[19] [20]

---

19 Early on a fine winter's morning I walked out of Santa Eulària, heading north-east along the coast path. At some point before I reached S'Argamassa, the sun rose, prompting this poem.
20 Poem also published in *Nature Writing* online magazine on 01/06/2018 (https://naturewriting.com/line-in-two-blues/).

Round Ferry Corner

Round the ferry corner, the smell
Of drying seaweed slaps me alert.
Memories of bladderwrack carpets,
Slippery on a pebbly beach.
We squeezed the slimy vesicles
To make them pop.
Draped fronds on our heads
To make a horrid, viscid wig.
I remember a composite
Of many seaweed carpets
On many pebbly beaches
From sunshine times of yore.
I strive to hold the salt, musty, fishy scent
Through cigarette smoke and cheap perfume
Of people passing by.
In vain. But maybe I'll walk
This way again.

Santa Eulària des Riu, January 2017.[21] [22]

---

21 A scent brings back fond, forgotten memories. The "ferry corner" is where
the small ferries dock in Santa Eulària.
22 Poem also published in *Nature Writing* online magazine on 25/06/2018
(https://naturewriting.com/round-ferry-corner/).

Magon's Rock

Magon's rock lying sombre,
Flat between stone-grey sea
And darkly brooding sky,
Like a great black beast
Quiet, semi-submerged:
The dragon I fancy,
Resting perhaps,
On its timely flight
Marking coming spring.
For look there, friends!
Almond has blossomed.

Pou d'es Lleo, Sant Carles de Peralta, February
2017.[23]

23 Tagomago is a small island just off the north-east coast of Ibiza. It is said its
name derives from that of one of the great Carthaginian general Hannibal's
brothers, Magón. Under Islamic rule it was known as Taj Umayu. Around
the time I walked by, despite the grey sky and the cool wind, the almonds
were just coming into blossom. In ancient China it was believed that spring
was brought by the passing of a dragon, and that the opening of blossom
that swept the country was a mark of its passing.

Crossroads

Standing at a crossing of paths;
paths of earth and rock that snake
through pine and thyme; and time.
A lattice of prints across the land.
This way to the hills.
That one to the bay.
This to the town,
and that to a thin blue line
a light year away.

See the pattern that marks our land!
The richly criss-cross weave,
the warp and weft, we left
in time and place; of men
and women's aims, and aimlessness.
From our beginning
to our today.
And tomorrow
whither goes the way?

Sant Vicent, Sant Joan de Labritja, March 2017.[24] [25]

---

24 From nearby Tanit's Cave in the hills above the tiny village of Sant Vicent, a small path leads down a wooded valley to a torrent bed, dry except after heavy rain. There it meets, and crosses, another path. Eivissa is criss-crossed by a myriad of such ancient paths.

25 Poem also published in *Nature Writing* online magazine on 05/10/2018 (https://naturewriting.com/crossroads/).

Morning's Coast

Dawn breaks on Morning's Coast
Orange-cream and pyric,
Of razor rocks, volcanic,
Like fair, terrible Tanit,
Who watches from her lair.

Sun up on Morning's Coast.
Silver glints off inky waves,
Like treasure lost in sunken caves
Of pirates brutal, rude and brave,
Whose breath still mists the air.

Wind falls on Morning's Coast
In bitter blasts or whispers mild,
Now playing coy, now yelling wild,
Now like the mother, now the child,
Now like a lover's touch so rare.

Sea up on Morning's Coast,
Brisk as joy, or white as death,
Breathing of the Levant breath,
Sculpting splendid ruggedness,
Of crumbling cliffs and boulders bare.

Land fall on Morning's Coast,
Men of Tiber and Phoenicia,
Weathered Argonauts tenacious,
Their gods both cruel and gracious,
Above them all, Tanit the fair.

Sant Vicent, Sant Joan de Labritja, March 2017.[26] [27]

---

26 Walking the north-east coast of Ibiza from Cap de Can Negret to S'Escullet, 8th March 2017. Tanit, Phoenician and Carthaginian goddess of war, motherly love, and fertility, looks down on this coastline from her cave-shrine high in the hills above.

27 Poem also published in *Nature Writing* online magazine on 30/04/2018 (https://naturewriting.com/mornings-coast/).

The End of the Road

Found under a stone at Punta des Far,
    Formentera ...

How did I end up here?
It's been a long road, it's true,
with many bends and forks,
and many landscapes too.
But now, if I look back,
the way is straight and dead and flat
as far as I can see.

This is, I think, the end of the road,
at a lighthouse car park,
on a lonely, treeless headland.
The taxi is now just a receding dot,
like so many things.

I walk the few remaining steps,
and sit.
Before me the sky and sea
stretch as one to infinity,
as flat as the morning,
as grey as the hole in my chest.
They seem to reach for me.

The morning is better for it, I'd said,
the evening would be just too dread.

How can the air be so still?
Expectant, as a void to fill.

Something must happen soon.
Far below in slow motion
whiteness blooms on jagged stone.
Anyone falling from this height
would smash to gory bits
of flesh and bone.
Not a pretty sight.
But I've always dreamed of flight.
So even here, even now,
I am capable of humour.
But am I of desperation?
Or if not, abandon?

I move a little closer.
take out a pencil, a scrap of paper
to write down these my thoughts.
For what?
Is this, then, the end of the road?

Santa Eulària des Riu, March 2017.[28] [29]

---

28 Sometimes one thinks, if it came to that, "How would I do it?" Personally, I've always dreamed of flying, but I've never liked spectators. Punta des Far, Formentera, in winter is a suitably dramatic yet secluded location to take flight for a few seconds, before the end.

29 First published in *Tears*, New York Literary Magazine, November 2017.

Nature's Healing Stuff

Yes, this truly is nature's healing stuff,

This symphony of colour and scent,

Live, alive, on the hills.

Soft unthinking joy is the healing way;

Doctor, you cannot separate it,

Bottled, to cure man's ills.

No remedy in your book compares one tenth

To the wild, glorious riot of life,

That here, mind and body fills.

Sant Vicent, Sant Joan de Labritja, March 2017.[30] [31]

---

30 Springtime is pure joy wandering over the Eivissa hillsides, with the island still fresh from winter rainfall and the wild flowers running riot with explosive energy.

31 Poem also published in *Nature Writing* online magazine on 14/09/2018 (https://naturewriting.com/natures-healing-stuff/).

Siesta Beach, 8th August, 7 a.m.

The world has had a sweaty, restless night.
A tangerine sun squints, befuddled, through
    the eastern haze.
A peevish sea jabs, in boredom, at brown
    weary rocks.
Leaden air paws, oppressive, regressive, at
    your prickly skin,
Makes you trip and swear. The world
Casts a cynic's eye, says there!

Not-so-old walls of cement and sea water
    submit
Passively to time and indifference.
Cracked, decaying, broken, dying, taking
Their pointless graffiti with them.
Palm fronds and cuttings from verdant
    gardens
Dumped here in blithe contempt.
They whine for respect but afford us none
And our dignity crumbles and falls
Like the broken, rotten walls.

A red, rough, stony path,
Scrubby verges of lank grass,
Plenty dog shit, much variety,
(Amongst cuttings from the topiary),
Fresh and soft; or rotting, old and dry,
In brown, black, green, dull grey, chalk white,
Competes for space with beer cans, plastic

> bags,
> Crisp packets, water bottles, torn up rags,
> Burger boxes, paper wrappings, ends of fags.
> Then concrete platforms built for bathing in
> > the sun,
> Abandoned all to flows of grime and mulch
> > and dung.

> And the sad dusty path is dry as bone,
> Except where a garden's dribbling hose
> Makes muddy puddles here and there, and
> > where
> You slip and fall and swear. The world
> Casts you a jaundiced glare, says there!
> You want to know how and you want to ask
> > why,
> But the world squeals deafening, shrill and
> > high,
> Like a festering sow in a foul pigsty.

Siesta, Santa Eulària des Riu, August 2017.[32]

---

32 A darkly cynical poem. One often hears it said or written about our home island that it is "paradise". In places it is extremely beautiful, in others it can inspire the kinds of sentiments expressed in this poem, written in a moment of negativity about the disrespect people sometimes show for their environment. But maybe I had just had a bad night.

As Near as We Will Ever Be Again

Over where the sky is brightening they'll be
    eating Yeung Chow
But this is just about as far from home as we
    can go
Yet we are as near as we will ever be again
And summer after summer hurtle by us like a
    train
Sitting on the sea wall here at daybreak with
    my wife
Silent, impassive, thoughts of fate, thoughts of
    life
Looking to the rising sun, transported on its
    rays
Born home a precious moment by the power
    of our gaze

Santa Eulària des Riu, September 2017.[33]

---

33 During the summer of 2017, when this poem was written, every day at dawn
when I went down to the beach to swim, a middle-aged Oriental couple
would be sitting on the concrete ledge below the sea wall, gazing out
towards the rising sun. I often wondered what they were thinking.

Out of Sight

Out of sight and out of mind
Is a saying for the blind
Who'll never cast a look
About this pretty little nook
You throw a bottle in the sea
In Barcelona, Beirut, Benghazi
And though it seems out of the way
It turns up here in this bay
Chuck it in the river, far away,
In Manchester or Mandalay
Though it's far and out of reach
It ends up here on this beach
This world's a mystery and it's magic
But when we wade through tides of plastic
The magic's black, and we, my friends,
Are tragic

Sant Miquel de Balansat, October 2017.[34]

---

34 If one walks about the coastline of Eivissa, one comes across many pretty little secret bays that can only be accessed on foot or by boat. Far from the beaten track, they have no beach concessions to clean them up, and very sadly, they are invariably strewn with mountains of plastic, most of which is water bottles. One thinks, if there is that much on one tiny beach, how much is floating around in the sea? And all of it was put there by human beings.

Chasm Between Worlds

I remember as it were a dream
This crevice upon the mount
This fissure into savage rock
Of deepness beyond count
This abyss unto the mystery heart
This shaft to the unknown
This passage to Eden's earthly bed
This breach in my here and now
This cut into the wall of sight
This chasm between the worlds
To where the flesh meets heart meets mind
And even chance the soul
Though not immortal, just a spark
For precious seconds before the dark

Santa Eulària des Riu, Eivissa, August 2018.[35]

---

35 While out walking I came across a deep crevice in a rocky outcrop at the top
of the cliff at Cap d'Albarca, Sant Mateu. It was this that sparked my
imagination.

About Robert Hale

"While still on the road, learner, hunter of icicles, drinker of
Khayyam's wine, some kind of healer."

Robert grew up in the south of England before seeking his fortune
in foreign lands. His home now is on beautiful Eivissa with his
beloved Clouds Woman, who keeps him grounded and disabuses
him of any notion that he might be in any way perfect. He makes
himself useful and earns a crust by providing health care to the
local community. He loves to spend time walking the woods, cliffs
and coastlines of his island home, and torturing some apology for
music out of his mandolin. He loves solitude, bodies of water,
forests, observing the beauty and the harshness of nature, and
(quixotically) pondering the imponderable mysteries of life.
Robert's poetry has been published in several respected poetry
magazines. He is inspired by the beauty and mystery of the world
around us, the natural environment, the human condition, and the
greatest motivator of them all, love. His first collection of verse,
No Better Time Than This, was published in February 2018. A
second collection, *The Storyteller of Isfahan*, is on track to be
published in early 2019.

59

Soledad Hale

Girl with a Yellow Ribbon

A little girl at a ribbon stall
Blue, pink or brown?
Yellow he said, to her surprise
And so she took it down

Ever since, her drawings she filled
With that bright and cheerful colour
And ever since, the clothes she chose
Would carry a touch of yellow

The girl with the yellow ribbon in her hair
A thousand steps in the world has come
But when, in the distance, he looks, she knows
She can make a thousand steps and one

Eivissa, March/September, 2018.

See Her Run

See her run -
Like the mustang on the plains
Running is the journey and the end
She runs for no other reason
Because that is what mustangs do

See her run -
A fresh wind on her face
A quickening of the pace
A breaking of the gait
She senses a journey begun
She feels the thrill, she runs
Her way and aim unknown

See her run -
The road is a teacher of many lessons
Patience
Not to set off at a mighty gallop
For then the pace will wane and die;
Frugality
For she who manages her energies will go far;
To embrace change
For even staying herself
She changes day by day;
To slow the thoughts
In order to learn
To listen
In order to feel the way

See her run -
Today she chooses paths untravelled
Tomorrow the old familiar route
Today she travels far
Tomorrow just around the block
Everything changes, nothing stays the same
For this she is not less than she was before
But more

See her run -
She gives herself to the rhythm
Impelling her ever on
The sound of footfall on the ground
Arms move in time
Balancing the stride
Carry her like power wings
And beat of heart that joins beat of step
Percussive harmony
And the wave that fills the lungs
Of life and vigour to blood and flesh
The pump of breaths hypnotic
The pulse ancestral
And cradled by it
She in turn
Cradles it within

See her run -
Her gesture of greatness, of power
Always, endlessly onwards
Immersed in rhythms
Witness to the world
To everyday wonders

Trees, birds, insects, flowers
In a different consciousness
Living what surrounds her
Living what arises within
The flows and fragments
Thoughts, images, emotions, sensations
Sometimes fast, sometimes slow
Sometimes painful
As if the running breath would rinse her out
Shake her from within
Her footfall on this earth her truth
And her reflection
Returning home a small rebirth

See her run -
Like the mustang on the plains
Who knows where?
She smiles inside
See her run
See her run

Eivissa, May/September 2018.[36]

---

36 Written in collaboration with Robert Hale.

About Soledad Hale

I walk through life feeling the depth of my steps, trying to find the heart of things. My connection with the Earth makes me seek art in all its forms, in nature and in movement. I love those long days of sunshine which I can breathe in, slowly, deeply. The sea, yoga, and horses are my passions. The thing that most makes me flourish is to feel tenderness and love surrounding me. My roots are my tribe. I feel people and life, and I have a particular connection with the wild feminine, and the feminine aspect of all things, which gifts wisdom, strength and compassion.

65

Christo Janus

You The-Me

Have you come from times past falling leaves of loneliness caught in an arid desert breeze, where tears are turned to stone that blind the pain? You only see The-Who-What I am of yesteryears in tears of day. Like vine climbs a tree from birth it is hard to break free from the shackles of a troubled mind. Who I am is what I am, what I am is that which speaks. Without, You would see all there is to be free. For Who I am of yesterday cannot replenish the morrow of being You-The-Me today, free. Like a bird apt to fly from of the tree, spread your wings and fly in conscious dreams to reality The-Me. Come come to The-Me be free, free from the vines that bind, free from the shackles of a trouble mind. Be free, be free…

Come to The-Me

Come come, come to The-Me above
mountainous trees through streams of
flickering silver, from moonlight beams, in
shades to emerald blues and greens, cascading
twisting, pirouetting Autumn's falling shining
leaves.

Come to The-Me, sweet the honey Bee, happy
to live the life of The-Me that new dawn
brings, of birds swooping high and low to
mid-between of angel whispers, fleeting in
morning's songs to sing.

Come take shade in the light of the Old Yew
Tree, it's hidden knowledge given
unconditionally, come rest upon the stone
once rolled away for thee and hail the breath
in breathe, to re-new in volition of a self
power willed to be, free.

Come follow, follow The-Me through
pollinated seeds of leaves, once fallen from on
high the tree, in a blink of eye across the
nights shadows of light, fly in-conscious
dreams to reality…

Free from the vines at last, pure white the
silver trumpet blast, driven through a brighter
shade of mossed, wet green grass.

Come come, come to The-Me that You might live, but do not scurry scurry my anxious friend, across the page written with-in, from start of finish… Begin.

A Rose of Poetic Prose

A rose of poetic pose I have for you
composed, sweet of that sent unto me, a love
red rose.

To unpickle peckle the unpeckable pecked,
pick off petals, pick one by one, each
unveiling to the inner revealings, of love's true
red love by a rose and fire your passions
heart-full fragrance, with a gift from the
perfumed rose of scent. Kiss softly each, her
intoxicating red moist velvet lips, in sips, as
she blushes your tongue in mouth watering
tastes, likened to a full bodied wine, scented
from rose petals picked, each kissed one by
one, loves you, loves you not, loves you....!!!?

From your fingers to your nose, art the scent
of a rose red love, with passion pose, you
pickled thought impossible to pick, with heart
full of your blossoming scent and send each
petal you kiss, to in-love that someone with
you.

Thank you to one of scent, that rosed red my
heart, and high up ascent her blossomed
beauty, sweet maleficent, bar any other name,
red love rose. And open to all interpretive
thought, including our own prickled peckled
thoughts of a pickle question posed, for an

answer. Answered with love.

Wordsworth

When conveying a treasure of words' worth, from the place within poetic lake of mind and the river of thoughts gush in-through, with an over flowing surge, in verse to speak, then stream their force to a gentle will, in brooks to form and consume of there, their true nature's Worth, then words of better form do take. For where other versely poets might rapidly force release and dam not, their rivered thoughts to verse, then just is their worth of words, that do wilt with speech. But of words' worth that trickles unforced, voice speaks out loud with a gentle swim and spawn of their form to birth awakened, their nature of mind, with a poetic sense to feel. And enriched is the ferry-fisher merchant's soul, their net-catch of versely truths, not by another, borrow'd or stolen name, seen or unseen, are seen by their varying nature of words' worth to convey, their forgotten treasured gift to receive of free, poetic speech. Something Wordsworth, Will embed in his day, to say, in all we have forgotten yet to know, from the place within poetic lake, of mind.

Once upon a Dawn, Chorus Call

Once upon a dawn, a certain kind of morn, the
me came to rise from slumber's pace, with a
ready steady mind to firmly foot one's
thoughts, rebellious in place, from the
unevolving waltzen dance that binds the
mind's eye to unawakening sleep.

Firmly awakened rebellious in thought,
voice cock-a-doodled, voluntary dawning my
mind to speak out loud each tread in step, with
affirmations to renew, that keep of a life no
more to ignore, who the what I am that cries
untorn from the yesteryears, of self-same
blame. And not more ignore, more than the me
can become, with each step, to further-forward
in pace, of onwards and upwards, that
outwards the inward of down side to up side.

With the inside seen, seen with outside of the
who the what I am, have had to sense to feel
to think or not, to be. Then you will hear of
seeing all that binds, the untorn tears. You can
hide the truth from humanity but humanity
cannot hide from truth, for righteousness
belongs not to humanity, humanity belongs to
the righteouness of truth.

That true of course. With a ready steady foot

loose fancy free, the me stepped to, prepared
with ready wings, to flying through the
unconscious mind, and high the lows to mid
between the southern plexus emotional mind.
And true the heart to course. From untorn
tears.

And as my mind eyed the years of unspent
tears, combined realities of emotional
mind flowed in rapid quick release.

Spirited by life's tears awakened of their sleep,
the me set off free, with wings spread far and
wide, in true course to sing. That certain kind
of morn. Once upon a dawn. To sing of you
the me.

In universal song, the me sings in spoken
poetry.

The me am walking, talking, of you. Yes the
me am living, breathing life, this song of truth.
The me of a course, coursed through, flying,
flying high, through into conscious the mind,
you the me, free.

The me am living, laughing, life-loving you.

Come hold my hand, to awaken, step firmly
with mind, to be ground. And we'll be
walking, talking, singing songs with dancing,
living life, to truth.

Then we'll be flying, fly high above, to green
the heart of the southern plexus, emotional
mind, of untorn tears, being who the what am
of you, yesteryears, to be free. Come now,
come be free.

Come sing, chorus through, with living,
laughing, life-loving you the me. Free.

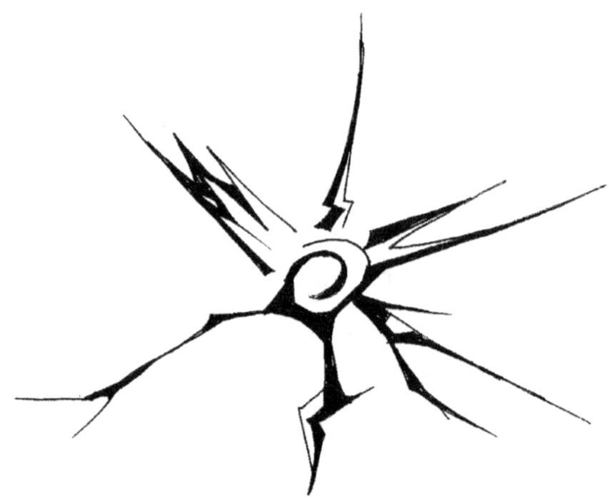

About Christo Janus

"If music be the soul of life, then philosophically, it could be said, through spoken lips, poetry imparts by blessed breath, nature's human words to form, the soul's vibrational life, the reason music exists to live for."

Born in Whitehawk Town, that I might live, that I might give, that I might receive. Brighton, a City of towns, where elm trees fill the city streets with fallen leaves, and her woodland parks shine brightly with my most beloved of all, the ever green yew tree. Brighton birthed the Whitehawk out of the me, to spread my wings and fly, across the Channel's rolling waves, to course through a new dawn. Although already travelled widely, this was another kind of leaving, where, in giving of myself, I received a life of freedom. I then spent several years involved in ecological projects in Spain, most recently in Ibiza where, among other things, I helped to design and dig a cave, taught permaculture, and created a forest refuge for all living things to share. I recently moved away, to Denmark, where I am restoring a small organic farm and looking after 60 happy chickens and 30 geese.

YABISA GASHOUSE

Loraine Parsons

Almond Snow

Almond snow falls.
Carpeting.
Winter thoughts.
Time for rebirth.
Springing.
Emerging hopes.

Santa Eulària des Riu, April 2018.

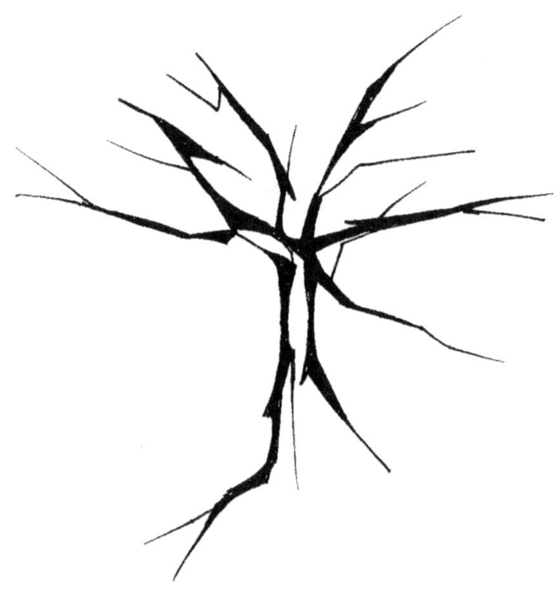

Goodbye Kate

Subconscious thoughts accompany me,
Enfolding me,
Caressing me.
Releasing me,
From an emptiness left by your death.

Stormtrooping the streets of London,
No more galleries, exciting eateries,
Up and down the underground,
From Brick Lane to the Eye,
No more Covent Garden,
No more fun in London.

A party of people swimming,
Around in the empty pool.
The alcohol freely flowing,
Laughter drowning out the fool.

Your stubborn determination,
That 40 a day would not kill you.
The cancer came and took your lungs,
Not satisfied it swept your brain and bones,
Your inevitable termination.

I slip back to my subconscious,
Enfolding you,
Caressing you,
Releasing you.
Good bye Kate.

Santa Eulària des Riu, April 2018.

The Rose

Your velvet petals pull me deep into your
    smell
Intoxicating thoughts overwhelm my senses
Ruby Red takes over, I am blinded by your
    colour
My fingers trace your lips into your soft sweet
    heart
As The Rose flows through my veins

Santa Eulària des Riu, September 2018.

Mean

Your jealousy
Withered me.
I died
I cried
Inside.
I lost my light,
From your paranoia I cowered,
I had to break perpetual night,
Leave my paradise behind.
I wandered lost into a void
Where emptiness stole off my mind
Our family torn apart,
You broke our golden daughter's heart.

Santa Eulària des Riu, November 2018.

About Loraine Parsons

Over forty years ago I arrived by boat to a magical island in the sun. I had found paradise on Earth. I lived in a small "casita" in the hills behind Benirrás beach. There was no electricity or running water, it wasn't important in the beginning. I lived with nature, up with the lark and oil lamps in the evening. Pulling full buckets of water from the well and walking everywhere were ways of staying healthy and fit. Mother Nature was kind to me, I learnt about the healing herbs that grew in abundance on the hill sides and we ate what was in season; another way of looking after yourself. Watching the morning mist clear from the flowing hills around Benirrás allowed me to welcome the new day with a joyful spirit. Smiling at my beautiful child as she played in the garden or taking walks to the beach for a dip in the sea. I was in heaven. I became more interested in the total beauty of the smallness in nature. I found that the inside of a shell or the heart of a rose cried out to me. My writing is very personal, coming from deep within me, showing my passions and emotions. On the other hand, it reflects my connections to the perfection of nature.

YABISA GASHOUSE

Youri Post

A Pathway Up

A pathway up disappears down the hill
Spider threads alongside lighting up in the
      silver sun
And the slow silent wind betrays its
      movement

See the opening of a flower and memories left
      behind

Two butterflies play with each other and the
      dry green
One laughs, one cries
And beside a wingless bird is being given to
      the ground
Yellow grey, its feather melt
as tears are taken by the earth
underneath we walk upon

Sant Rafel de sa Creu, April 2015.

Life Goes On, So They Say

Life goes on, so they say.
And although you always find a road to take
There'll always be some pain you leave behind
Sadness swells and sets on, you know
And then,
Suddenly you can feel it happening in your
      eyes
It flows over, and just for a moment, it's free
And gone again while you breathe

Sant Josep de Sa Talaia, June 2015.

Almost Dawn

It's almost dawn
It's not far any more
Overlooking the hills
A life ahead in the distance

Walking in between lands
With nothing but a stick to touch the ground

My feet turn cold

The last glow of the moon weeping

My ankles slowly dragging through pools of
    mud
And silhouettes standing still along the
    riverside

I see shadows of my loved ones
And the boy I once was, smiling,
guiding me away from the dark side of the
    road
And the noise of a life left behind

Ben Bulben, Ireland, February 2016.

In a Whisper so Quiet

That lonely winter night
When you slept without a dream
I came near
In a whisper so quiet
That only you could hear

It was almost left unnoticed
But you trembled
As if a bleak wind moved through your
        window frame
And caressed your half naked skin with soft
        intentions

And there
In the serene resting of your waking eyes
I saw, where I for all this time was looking for
But had lost somewhere along the way

So now, I just keep following the western
        wind
And call your name into the void in vain
If I can come home to you

Amsterdam, long ago.

The Northern Wind

The northern wind howls at my door
and the half light of the moon appears
      through
A life of robbing and stealing in a broken
      heart got me here

And now, it seems like nothing ever happened
      while I sing the old blues
and take the journey away from my cabin
      window
which is falling apart too like everything else
      does

- You've got to walk that lonesome valley
Well you gotta go by yourself
Well there ain't nobody else gonna go there
      for you
You gotta go there by yourself -

And believe it or not, I am a fulfilled man
but I only write when I'm sad

As the clouds are closing in
and I lay down on the cold ploughed ground
where I plough from dark till dark
and wonder, about how suffering leads to
      redemption

And at the same time, I think and feel:
What does it matter?
It makes no difference anyway.

The bird eats the ants
and the ants eat the bird when it has died.
We all find difficulties when we are happy
and happiness when difficulties arise.

What is there more to say?

Except that now the winter blue is dwelling
and everyone I love melting with the morning
      frost into the sun

Silhouettes of gold and silver around the
      leaves
where my breath condenses with and draws a
veil between all I ever know and what it is to
      see,
while I reach out to you
and see the dawn changing for something else
      to arrive

Something else, which is beyond all
but finds a way in
somehow

Nostra Senyora de Jesús, March 2016.[37]

---

37 *You've got to walk that lonesome valley etc.* This verse is from an American traditional spiritual song known as, among other titles, *Lonesome Valley.* These lyrics are in the public domain.

The Sunned Sea

The sunned sea whitens the horizon
Against the light of dusk which gathers an
      embrace
And at the same time there is a sense of
      leaving
Now that a boat of sails is drifting off into a
      starless night
Darkening the mountains and all the threats
      that lie ahead

With no direction home, I continue
Just like you
Till only the remnants of loneliness remain

English Channel, 2013.

There Is a Sadness

In my heart
There is a sadness
Which welcomes the world
And my body being fragile
Reminds me that I'm no different
from anything else that passes through
For also I will let go one day
Like a withered leaf on an autumn branch
That hardly meets the wind

Now say goodbye to a life lived
To the Earth, who has been my witness all
       along
And to all of you who gave me life
My loved ones
I will say goodbye, put my hands together
and bow for your presence when I sometimes
       was not

The masks I wore
I will lay aside for one last time
As if they are my evening clothes

And then, when I will be laying in my bed
And death arrives in my glazed eyes
And the pace of my heart slows down
Turning my body colder and colder
Grasping for air
It will be then that I finally have to let go
Of everything I thought was real

Or maybe, maybe not
I don't know
Maybe I'll stay
Holding the last moment with a light touch of
        regret
that life is fleeting

As is now
The last few drops of dew in the morning
        grass
And my footsteps disappearing when the sun
        climbs higher

Dechen Chöling, March 2017.

Late Night Rain Falls Heavy

Late night rain falls heavy
With nothing but a bag over my left shoulder
and tears on the letter in the pocket on my
      right

Walking into a town that won't have me
Wet on the cold stone pavement outside of the
      train station

Closing my eyes trying to sleep an hour or
      two
before I'll be on my way again
following all the sorrows beating in my heart

Just this morning we made love -
your endless beautiful and precious body
      buried into mine
And your skin
feeling like a long, long home
And in your eyes
I recognise the coming of spring

And then... then we said goodbye,
I left, turned around,
and saw you disappearing into the distance of
      a dream
Waking me up every time you touch me,
and appear again when the robin lands at my
      feet,
sees me, and flies off,

again, and again
into the same dream,
We meet

Dechen Chöling, March 2017.

It's Difficult to Write to You

One and a half years later...

It's difficult to write to you
as beautiful as you are
This pencil in my hand trembling on the
      folded white paper
will lead me to hurt
As immense that it can only be compared with
love

With the love we shared
and with the love we continue to share
Although across distance,
both our bodies still contained
in the longing to something beyond the body

A faint memory of nights we cried tears of
      coming home
when we moved into each other

In between all the fiery and painful struggles
we sometimes moved softer and more slow
till we almost didn't move any more,
our burning flesh melting,
our blood flowing and throbbing as one,
our breath silenced, so quiet
I became frightened in your eyes,
small as a child

I died, I was born again

shivering, naked in your arms
We arrived into each other
but I couldn't stay
I betrayed you
Not with the other women I spend my cold
       and lonely nights with,
but by closing my heart from you

I wasn't able yet to hold it in front of me
and honour you with it

As I realise now
that I'm on my knees,
in this labyrinth of beauty

My head bended down and my hands
digging the dry earth
And the only freedom
is that I never had it

Barcelona, August 2018.

About Youri Post

Asked to write a short bio...

I don't think a lot of words are necessary here, but if something is to be shared about me... I could just as well mention something about you, 'cause I ain't no different.

Pere Vergés
Coma

Me and the Poet

Now, me and the Poet
Were looking down
Standing on the balcony
At the break of dawn

Coming from the loneliness
And into the wild of old
Flowed a stream of words
For the free to behold

Then, lightning strikes
In the valley below
And we glimpse at the truth
Dancing with the waterfall

Now, me and the Poet
We both take a bow
With a farewell wish of joy
It is time for us to go

Santa Agnès de Corona, March 2018.

Heart of Whale

If I can sleep on the ground
And my sun rises at night
The earth is all dressed in colours
As it travels through my hands
And the blue of the sea is so sweet
As it sinks behind the pines

I live in the heart of a whale
That on the beaches did fall asleep
If death finds me on my back
And my picture's a wounded heel
For me don't you weep and wail
Now I'm the flowers on the tree

I am the son of a siren
And my desire comes from the flame
Salt and white earth I'll leave you
Remembrance of the ancient ways
My hands are cracked like stone
Where forgotten rivers lay

Santa Agnès de Corona, March 2018.

The Witch

Life is fast, death is slow
You stand alone at sunset
Waiting waiting waiting

It never was your concern
Just how far you would go
You were always there

And the grass comes and goes
With the sun, with the rain
And the wind blows

Then comes the night
What is there to know?
Life is fast, death is slow

Santa Agnès de Corona, March 2018.

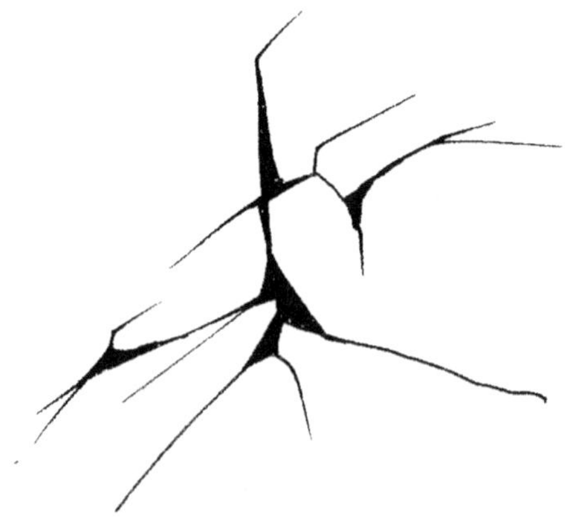

The Fair

Hear the lightning split the sky
A little girl alone at the gates
The fair is closing down
The evening birds no longer fly
With a broken toy in her hand she waits
And darkness sleeps underground

Take my hand but I must let go
A distant call and it begins to rain
A wish, a smile, but wait a while
Looking back at this house of woe
The morning lights the night again
The merry-go-round and the carousel smile

Little girl walking in the rain
Your shoes got stuck in the muddy ground
And your footprints were washed away
Afternoon the fair is open once again
Colours flashing turning round and round
Crowds they come and go and never stay

Santa Agnès de Corona, April 2018.

Ode to Findhorn

What did you bring
From the land of rain
Where the days be long
And the mountains green?

The sun rises over northern skies
An easy breeze moves
Across Findhorn's sleepy eyes

Somewhere out there
The world's unending fair
Just a bird in the morning light
Will sing alone without a care

Slowly crimson colours
Paint ever so faintly
The thin watery clouds
A hopeful blue I see
And here it comes…the sun

The sea is rough by the pirate's grave
"No one was saved"
I heard the wind sing to the brave

Loneliness drifts into the empty church
Where no one prays,
Gone are those days to sweet decay
And so regains the moss
The stones engraved

Asleep they fall
They heed the call
That cares no more
For who was saved

The tides round the stones
Uncover the sands
And Man?
He comes and goes

The mighty matron
Announced with a smile
No visitors allowed!

And the trees grow high
So keep your secrets not on bark
For the tree will fall
And the deer glides
Along the broken shades
And the Lady keeps the dark

Painted leaves swim the creeks
Many dreams away from Moray Firth
For all that lives is gone to earth
And shapes that be the coming birth

Santa Agnès de Corona, April 2018.

Rocking Chair

You make me cry
Sometimes
If I stare too hard

You cast shadows
All over
You the shadow-less one

You keep me warm
Set my breath on fire
No words can reach you
Not even anything
At all

Just like the silence
All over
Casting shadows of sound

Who are you?
Nameless, formless and less
And less

But I just could not make it
Without you
Nor anything
At all

My grandfather's on the rocking chair
And I'm sitting on his knees

And he says to me
There, there it is
The Sun

It was always there

Santa Agnès de Corona, May 2018.

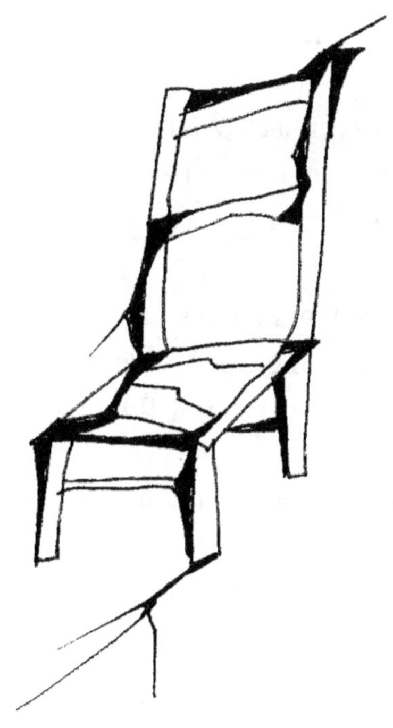

Maybe

My grandad said to me:
If I make it through wintertime
Then maybe next season I´ll be free

And if I lose my breath today
Keeping time with the gentle play
Then maybe…………

And if I stay here long enough
And reach that misty mountain path
Then maybe………

And if I´d never seen your face
Would that change my place in space
Then maybe……

And when sadness comes to fill your soul
Silent mother the ground is cold
Then maybe next season I´ll be free

Santa Agnès de Corona, June 2018.

Sweetheart in Pain

As your heart burns away
With the flute that you played
And we'll never know
Until we meet again
On the banks of the rivers
Of blood with no name

We did try to love
And we lost every gain
And the woman in you
Was never the same
You died in the garbage
Of faraway lands

Now your hand is cold
All that remains is gold
And now you have gone
To the sweet ways beyond
May your heart be bold
With the beauty you hold

Who am I?
I am your ancient lover
The one always lost
A sweetheart in pain

Santa Agnès de Corona, August 2018.

Transfigurations

And now that I see how they fall
From your eyes your slaves and all
And your instant has been lost
All around the light that was

You cannot find him by your side
From you now your child did hide
At midnight on the temple steps
He took your idols you don't forget

Your face is frozen for a while
Beneath a veil you keep a smile
Your memories they hold no claims
And in your lovers no fire remains

Instant changes you can see
All those cries upon the seas
Transfigurations of ancient songs
I heard the light of birds alone

Fishermen lay down their traps
Solitary, strange and dark
Their nets are only deeper thoughts
Brave the silence that was caught

Santa Agnès de Corona, August 2018.

Glow

Watching the wrecks wash up on the shores
Where the songs will return in a bliss
On faraway days of befores
Forever the end of the game
And yet the sun did not burn
As we rode in search of the grail
I don't really want to know all about you
Just let the breezes blow like the stars that
      glow
Anyway
We saw sirens fly through the night
Heavens arise in their sleep
And the rainbows made love to me
And the songs of freedom were sweet
And I played my harp to the wind
But already the rivers did weep

Santa Agnès de Corona, September 2018.

The Moment

I lived in the moment
My life passed in a moment
My tears of birth were still flowing
As I laid down my staff

I looked up at the tree
I did climb to the top
Uncertain at the highest branch
Letting go, but holding on
Remembering who I was
Or who I will be
Not a bird
Not a stone
Not a tree
Sometimes it's just too hard to agree
Or disagree
If I fall like a bird
I will be a stone
Looking up to the tree

Walking back to the ruins
Beauty falls all around
And I cry myself back into the world
The world, the world
Whatever that may be

The flowers on my porch
They come and go
Floating shadows into my room

Because the will of the sun
Because the will of the wind
And beyond, and beyond

The cries of the wild in the woods
Still alive and unknown
You cannot hear the scream of the land
Torn apart by the dream
Asleep and struck by grief
And the spider weaves across the leaves
And right there it lives

Santa Agnès de Corona, October 2018.

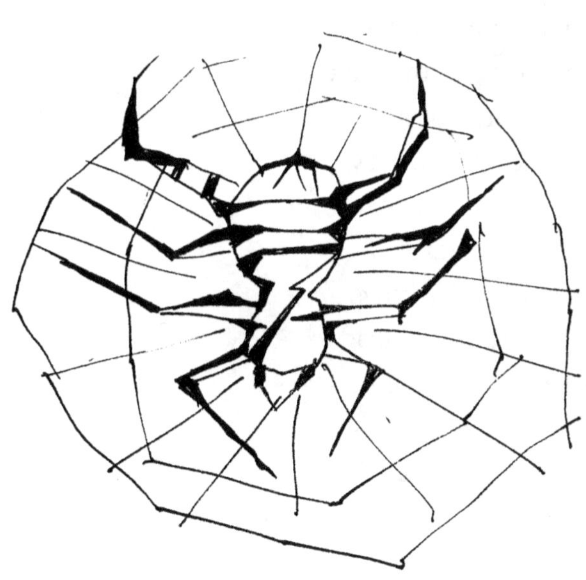

Ode to Es Vedrà

Es Vedrà dragon asleep
In the sky of your night
Your spirit I heed

My boat on the rocks
Away from the tide
I have bared my feet
Set fire on your hide

Your drums are of stone
To show me the way
A madness of old
If you do your own way

Your watery flutes
The voice in the cave
The chords of a lute
A child gone astray

Rats and lizards
Seagulls and crows
Alive from the dead
A sacrifice untold

I fly through the air
Far from witches and chains
I cut through the land
The father of extremes

Your thirst of the blue
Is burning your trees
Your skin is in wrinkles
Like the light on the sea

Your fire knows of mysteries
Springs born of the wind
Dry streams of blood
Of a world lost in sin

Your heart is intense
Your summer is flame
Foam and the truth
Like the river you crave

Santa Agnès de Corona, October 2018.

Around the World

In the streets of Paris where the clochard
     makes his rounds
The iron tower is the new man's Notre Dame
Around the world where the horizon meets the
     sky on the ice
They canned the air of Alaska for the blind
The stuffed white bear with the glass and teary
     eyes looks quite alive
I am leaving in the morning of my life
I kept her in my heart but she moved along
     with change
I believe the Weaver's calling is so pure and
     strange

Dusty bible blue downtown Tokyo grey
Buddha smiles a Nara sunny day
Father Brown plays the accordion with a smile
     before the graves
Sister Marian is crying for my fate
Compassion serves the sake as the monks of
     Kyoto play
The mind has many riddles come my way
She never said she would wait forever but she
     did for a long long time
How could I forget her? …She was just one of
     a kind

American tramp in Delhi laughing takes my
     hand
Spent the night with the junkies in the heights
Angels came to save me when I broke down

and cried
Sent me down to Keinchi in the light
The river yogi will eat his chicken when he
gets back home
Now he's in the jungle's bed of stone
I'm sorry that my letters got lost between the
songs
It took us a whole of a lifetime to know our
love was strong

I crossed the mountains with many a friend
but now I'm all alone
In Nainital the Saint bids me along
I stay and he rows forever and the water draws
the sound
A frozen moment that was never found
In Kathmandu I crossed between my eyes the
fearless grounds
Amen I cried and love is coming down
I hear your voices, dreams of time, your mind
so far beyond
Now my guitar is broken and I must carry on

Krishnamurti's back in town with his sad and
freedom songs
God's prasad is there before you fly
To Jerusalem where the golden calf is still
well and alive
The blood that was spilt it never dried
And I'm tired and I'm alive and I died and I
cried
And I'm coming home and my clothes are all
white
Never mind my love I don't know who am I

It's a simple world to live in when all your
love's alive

Santa Agnès de Corona, November 2018.

Reflections on THE A

The Sea, The Sky, The Sun, The Moon
Any moment or The Moment
I live in a room, it is The Room
A torment, The Torment

Some say the cracks are many
But the Ineffable is but one
Try to explain and it's just funny
Many strings and a chord is strum

My symphony needs a chord,
The Chord
I search like I do The Word
New to me and unheard

A crack is but a small crack
Of the Crack
I'm quite sure the lazy lizard
Will not mind the light of day
Of The Sun's many a ray

Evening comes and it is cold
To each his own
We light A Fire
We light The Fire

Santa Agnès de Corona, November 2018.[38]

---

38 We had a little debate about the title of this book. The original suggestion
was "The Crack...", but eventually "A Crack" prevailed. Pere, though, was
not convinced!

About Pere Vergés Coma

Born in Barcelona 1953 in the Garden of the Sun. The hands of the gardener were like the bark of the trees, the colour of the pine nuts in the clay pot. The magic of words and songs, the low tides and the pools, the master with the eyes of a hawk, faraway lands, the touch of those hands, happiness and pain, sunny days and heavy rain, the shattered doors of the temple, and this white island of today. Here where the enchanted gulls swirled over me in a heavenly dance turning their given screams into impossible choirs of musical bliss.